Masters of Deceit: Double Agents and the Dangerous Game of Counterintelligence

Copyright Page

TITLE: Masters of Deceit: Double Agents and the Dangerous Game of Counterintelligence

1ST Edition

Copyright @ 2023

ISBN: 9798223333401

Table of Contents

Masters of Deceit: Double Agents and the Dangerous Game of Counterintelligence

By Roberto Miguel Rodriguez

Book Outline

In this book, we delve into the intricate world of double agents and the dangerous game of counterintelligence. Whether you are a history enthusiast, a lover of spy thrillers, a political junkie, or simply someone intrigued by the secrets and mysteries of espionage, this chapter will captivate your imagination.

Cold War Espionage Stories: The Intricate World of Double Agents during the Cold War Era

The Cold War era was a time of heightened tension between the United States and the Soviet Union, characterized by a relentless battle for supremacy in intelligence gathering. In this section, we explore the lives of double agents who played a pivotal role in shaping history during this tumultuous period.

Historical Espionage Stories: Unveiling the Lives of Double Agents Throughout History

Espionage is not a phenomenon limited to the Cold War era. In this section, we take a step back in time and uncover the captivating stories of double agents throughout history. From ancient civilizations to modern times, these agents have infiltrated enemy ranks, manipulated leaders, and altered the course of nations.

Spy Thriller Espionage Stories: High-Stakes Adventures of Double Agents in the Modern World

If you crave high-octane action and heart-pounding suspense, this section is tailor-made for you. We unravel real-life spy thriller stories where double agents risked everything in daring missions that could change the course of world events. From shadowy meetings to thrilling escapes, these stories will keep you on the edge of your seat.

Political Espionage Stories: Double Agents in the Realm of International Politics

Politics and espionage have always been intertwined. In this section, we explore the treacherous world of double agents operating within the realm of international politics. From infiltrating governments to manipulating elections, these agents played a dangerous game, serving multiple masters while trying to protect their own interests.

Technological Espionage Stories: The Secret Lives of Double Agents in the Cyber Age

As technology advances, so does the world of espionage. In this section, we delve into the covert operations of double agents in the cyber age. From hacking into secure systems to stealing classified information, these agents navigate the digital realm with finesse, leaving no trace behind.

Femme Fatale Espionage Stories: Double Agents and the Art of Seduction

Throughout history, femme fatales have used their charm and seduction to extract secrets and manipulate powerful men. In this section, we explore the captivating stories of female double agents who mastered the art of seduction, using their beauty and wit to deceive even the most vigilant adversaries.

Espionage Stories: Double Agents and the Dangerous Game of Counterintelligence

The world of espionage is a dangerous one, where betrayal lurks around every corner. In this section, we delve into the treacherous world of double agents and the deadly game of counterintelligence. From unmasking moles to foiling enemy operations, these agents risked their lives to protect their countries.

Espionage Stories: Double Agents and the Treacherous World of Undercover Operations

Undercover operations require immense skill, courage, and the ability to blend seamlessly into enemy territory. In this section, we explore the stories of double agents who went deep undercover, adopting false identities and risking exposure at every turn. Their bravery and resourcefulness will leave you in awe.

No matter your interest in espionage, this subchapter presents a collection of captivating stories that span different eras and niches within the realm of double agents and counterintelligence. Prepare to be enthralled by the dangerous world of spies and their daring exploits.

Chapter 1: The Cold War Era: A Breeding Ground for Double Agents

The Origins of the Cold War

In the aftermath of World War II, the world witnessed a new kind of conflict that would shape the course of history for decades to come – the Cold War. This subchapter delves into the origins of this ideological confrontation between the United States and the Soviet Union, exploring the key events and factors that led to the escalation of tensions.

The seeds of the Cold War were sown long before the end of World War II. As the war drew to a close, the ideological differences between the two superpowers became increasingly apparent. The United States championed democracy, capitalism, and individual freedoms, while the Soviet Union embraced communism and advocated for a classless society. These opposing worldviews set the stage for a struggle for global dominance.

One of the critical turning points was the division of Germany and Europe into separate spheres of influence. The Soviets sought to exert control over Eastern Europe, establishing communist governments in countries like Poland, Hungary, and Czechoslovakia. This led to growing concerns among Western powers about Soviet expansionism and the spread of communism.

Another significant event was the dropping of atomic bombs on Hiroshima and Nagasaki by the United States. This display of nuclear power not only ended the war but also ushered in a new era of fear and uncertainty. The development of atomic weapons became a central focus for both superpowers, leading to an arms race that defined much of the Cold War.

Espionage played a crucial role during this period, with double agents navigating the treacherous world of counterintelligence. These spies infiltrated government agencies, military establishments, and scientific institutions to gather vital information. Their high-stakes adventures and dangerous missions became the stuff of legends, captivating audiences around the world.

The geopolitical landscape also played a significant role in fueling the Cold War. The United States and the Soviet Union engaged in a series of proxy wars, supporting opposing sides in conflicts such as the Korean War and the Vietnam War. These conflicts served as battlegrounds for the superpowers' ideological struggle, further escalating tensions and heightening the risk of a nuclear confrontation.

As the world entered the cyber age, espionage took on new dimensions. Technological advancements enabled double agents to operate in the shadows of the digital realm, engaging in cyber warfare and stealing sensitive information. The dangers of espionage expanded beyond physical borders, highlighting the growing importance of cybersecurity.

The origins of the Cold War were complex and multi-faceted, shaped by ideological differences, geopolitical maneuvering, and the shadowy world of espionage. This subchapter offers a glimpse into this tumultuous period, inviting readers to uncover the intricate web of double agents, political maneuvering, and high-stakes adventures that defined the era. Whether you are a fan of cold war espionage stories, historical espionage tales, or spy thrillers set in the modern world, the origins of the Cold War provide a gripping narrative that continues to captivate audiences today.

The Role of Espionage in the Cold War

Espionage played a pivotal role in shaping the course of the Cold War, an era defined by intense ideological rivalry and global power struggles between the United States and the Soviet Union. In "Masters of Deceit: Double Agents and the Dangerous Game of Counterintelligence," we delve into the intricate world of double agents during this tumultuous period, exploring their lives, adventures, and the treacherous game of counterintelligence they engaged in.

During the Cold War, both superpowers recognized the strategic importance of intelligence gathering. Espionage became a primary tool in their arsenal, as they sought to gather information on each other's military capabilities, political intentions, and technological advancements. Double agents played a crucial role in this dangerous game, infiltrating enemy organizations and feeding valuable information back to their handlers.

Historical espionage stories, such as those from World War II, set the stage for the Cold War era. The exploits of double agents like Kim Philby, Aldrich Ames, and Oleg Penkovsky captivated the public as their lives were unveiled, revealing the immense risks they took and the high stakes involved. These stories captured the imagination of readers, as they showcased the intricate web of deception and betrayal that characterized the world of double agents.

In the modern world of spy thrillers, the role of double agents remains as relevant as ever. With advancements in technology, espionage has evolved into the realm of cyberspace. Technological espionage stories take readers into the secret lives of double agents who operate in the cyber age, navigating complex networks and engaging in high-stakes adventures to gather classified information.

Political espionage stories shed light on the role of double agents in international politics. These agents, often operating at the highest levels of government, play a crucial role in shaping policy decisions and influencing global events. Their actions have the potential to alter the course of history, as they navigate the treacherous world of undercover operations and constantly weigh the risks and rewards of their actions.

Femme fatale espionage stories explore the art of seduction as a tool in the double agent's arsenal. These agents use their charm and allure to extract information from unsuspecting targets, highlighting the dangerous game of manipulation and deceit they engage in to achieve their objectives.

In "Masters of Deceit: Double Agents and the Dangerous Game of Counterintelligence," we immerse ourselves in the thrilling world of espionage. Through the lens of double agents, we uncover the secrets, dangers, and moral complexities that defined the Cold War era and continue to shape the world of intelligence gathering today. Whether you are a history enthusiast, a lover of spy thrillers, or simply intrigued by the treacherous world of undercover operations, this subchapter offers a captivating exploration of the role of espionage during the Cold War.

The Double Agent Phenomenon

In the shadows of espionage history, a breed of spies exists whose actions and allegiance constantly teeter on the edge of treachery and loyalty. They are the double agents, masters of deceit who play a dangerous game of counterintelligence. In the book "Masters of Deceit: Double Agents and the Dangerous Game of Counterintelligence," we delve into the intricate world of these enigmatic figures, exploring their lives and the impact they had on the course of history.

During the Cold War era, the world witnessed a surge in double agent activity. The stakes were high, and the consequences of betrayal could mean the difference between victory and defeat. Cold War Espionage Stories: The Intricate World of Double Agents during the Cold War Era uncovers the hidden stories of these double agents, revealing the risks they took and the games they played to outmaneuver their enemies.

But the phenomenon of double agents did not start nor end with the Cold War. Throughout history, individuals have chosen to walk the tightrope of loyalty, betraying their countries in favor of foreign powers. Historical Espionage Stories: Unveiling the Lives of Double Agents Throughout History takes readers on a journey through time, exploring the lives of double agents from ancient civilizations to present-day conflicts, revealing the motivations and consequences of their actions.

In the modern world, the game of espionage has evolved, and so have the double agents. Spy Thriller Espionage Stories: High-Stakes Adventures of Double Agents in the Modern World delves into the thrilling adventures of spies who navigate the complex web of information warfare, technological advancements, and political intrigue. From cyber espionage to cutting-edge undercover operations, these double agents walk a perilous tightrope, risking their lives for the greater good.

The realm of international politics is not devoid of double agents either. Political Espionage Stories: Double Agents in the Realm of International Politics uncovers the murky world of political espionage, where allegiances shift with the wind and trust is a rare commodity. From infiltrating political parties to manipulating elections, these double agents play a dangerous game that can shape the destiny of nations.

As technology advances, so does the world of espionage. Technological Espionage Stories: The Secret Lives of Double Agents in the Cyber Age explores the dark side of the digital world, where double agents exploit vulnerabilities and manipulate information. From hacking government systems to sabotaging critical infrastructure, these double agents utilize their technological prowess to wreak havoc on their enemies.

But not all double agents are men. Femme Fatale Espionage Stories: Double Agents and the Art of Seduction uncovers the intricate interplay between seduction and espionage. These female double agents utilize their charm and allure to extract valuable information and manipulate their targets. From Mata Hari to modern-day femme fatales, their stories reveal the power of seduction as a weapon in the game of counterintelligence.

Espionage is a dangerous game, and double agents are at the heart of its treacherous world. Espionage Stories: Double Agents and the Dangerous Game of Counterintelligence explores the intricate web of deception, betrayal, and danger that surrounds these enigmatic figures. From the motivations that drive them to the risks they take, this subchapter uncovers the untold stories of double agents and their impact on the world of espionage.

In the treacherous world of undercover operations, double agents hold a unique position. Espionage Stories: Double Agents and the Treacherous World of Undercover Operations uncovers the hidden lives of these spies who operate in the shadows, risking everything to gather intelligence and protect their true identities. From deep cover assignments to high-stakes infiltrations, their stories reveal the true extent of their bravery and sacrifice.

In "Masters of Deceit: Double Agents and the Dangerous Game of Counterintelligence," we explore the captivating world of double agents. From the Cold War era to the present day, these spies have shaped the course of history, leaving a lasting impact on the world of espionage. Whether you are fascinated by Cold War espionage stories, historical intrigue, or the dangerous world of undercover operations, this book offers a unique glimpse into the lives of double agents and the dangerous game they play.

Unveiling the Lives of Cold War Double Agents

The cold war era was a time of intense political tension and global conflict, with the world divided between the United States and the Soviet Union. In this dangerous landscape, a group of individuals known as double agents emerged, playing a treacherous game of counterintelligence that would have far-reaching consequences. In "Masters of Deceit: Double Agents and the Dangerous Game of Counterintelligence," we delve deep into the lives of these enigmatic figures, uncovering their secrets, motivations, and the high-stakes adventures they embarked upon.

Cold War Espionage Stories: The Intricate World of Double Agents during the Cold War Era.

As the world stood on the brink of nuclear war, double agents were at the forefront of the clandestine battle between East and West. Our book takes you on a thrilling journey through the intricate world of double agents, revealing how they operated within intelligence agencies, passing on vital information while simultaneously deceiving their handlers. From the infamous Cambridge Five to lesser-known figures, their stories shed light on the dangerous world of espionage during the Cold War.

Historical Espionage Stories: Unveiling the Lives of Double Agents Throughout History.

While the Cold War provided a fertile ground for double agents, their existence predates this era. "Masters of Deceit" explores the lives of double agents throughout history, from ancient times to World War II and beyond. By examining their motivations, loyalties, and the risks they took, we gain a deeper understanding of the intricate web of espionage that has shaped world events.

Spy Thriller Espionage Stories: High-Stakes Adventures of Double Agents in the Modern World.

Espionage is not confined to the pages of history; it continues to thrive in the modern world. Our book brings you thrilling spy thriller stories of double agents operating in the twenty-first century. With a focus on high-stakes adventures, we uncover the dangerous missions, close calls, and heart-pounding moments that defined the lives of these double agents.

Political Espionage Stories: Double Agents in the Realm of International Politics.

Double agents often found themselves entangled in the complex web of international politics, where loyalties and alliances were constantly shifting. "Masters of Deceit" delves into the political intrigue surrounding these double agents, exploring how their actions influenced major political events and shaped the course of history.

Technological Espionage Stories: The Secret Lives of Double Agents in the Cyber Age.

As technology advances, so does the world of espionage. The book reveals the secret lives of double agents in the cyber age, where hacking, surveillance, and digital warfare are the tools of the trade. By examining their role in the world of technological espionage, we gain insight into the ever-evolving nature of intelligence gathering.

Femme Fatale Espionage Stories: Double Agents and the Art of Seduction.

The allure of espionage is often intertwined with tales of seduction and manipulation. "Masters of Deceit" shines a light on the fascinating stories of female double agents, exploring how they used their charm and cunning to extract information from their targets. These femme fatales played a crucial role in the world of counterintelligence, their stories serving as a testament to the power of deception.

Espionage Stories: Double Agents and the Dangerous Game of Counterintelligence.

The dangerous game of counterintelligence is at the heart of our book. We delve into the thrilling world of double agents, exploring the risks they took, the sacrifices they made, and the impact they had on global events. From the moles within intelligence agencies to the master manipulators, their stories are a testament to the enduring allure and treacherous nature of espionage.

Espionage Stories: Double Agents and the Treacherous World of Undercover Operations.

Undercover operations are the heart and soul of the double agent's world. "Masters of Deceit" pulls back the curtain on these treacherous operations, revealing the lengths to which double agents went to gain the trust of their enemies. By examining their covert operations, we gain a deeper understanding of the dangerous world of undercover espionage and the individuals who risked everything for their cause.

In "Masters of Deceit: Double Agents and the Dangerous Game of Counterintelligence," we unlock the secrets of these enigmatic figures, providing an enthralling read for the public and enthusiasts of Cold War espionage stories, historical espionage, spy thrillers, political and technological espionage, femme fatale stories, and the treacherous world of undercover operations.

Chapter 2: Double Agents Throughout History: From Ancient Times to the World Wars

Espionage in Ancient Times

Espionage, the art of gathering secret information, has a long and intriguing history that dates back to ancient times. In this subchapter, we will delve into the fascinating world of ancient spies and double agents, uncovering the secrets and techniques they employed to gain an upper hand in the treacherous game of counterintelligence.

Throughout history, various civilizations have utilized espionage as a means to gain an advantage over their enemies. From the cunning spies of ancient Egypt to the masterful double agents of the Roman Empire, the art of espionage has evolved and adapted to the changing times.

In ancient Egypt, Pharaohs relied on a network of spies to gather information about neighboring kingdoms and potential threats. These spies, known as "eyes and ears," infiltrated enemy territory, posing as traders or diplomats, and reported back valuable intelligence to their Pharaoh. Their knowledge often proved vital in safeguarding the kingdom against potential invasions.

The Roman Empire, too, had its share of skilled spies and double agents. These individuals, known as "speculatores," were trained in the arts of disguise and deception. They would assume false identities, infiltrate enemy camps, and gather information about military tactics and troop movements. Their intelligence was crucial in shaping the outcome of battles and ensuring the empire's dominance.

Espionage in ancient times was not limited to military intelligence alone. Spies were also employed for political purposes. In ancient China, for example, the concept of "Moles" emerged during the Warring States period. These double agents infiltrated rival states and worked undercover to sow discord and gather information. Their actions often played a significant role in the political landscape of the time.

The techniques employed by ancient spies may seem rudimentary compared to modern-day espionage, but their impact cannot be underestimated. From using hidden messages to relying on their wit and charm, these brave individuals risked their lives to serve their nations and change the course of history.

As we delve deeper into the world of espionage, it becomes evident that the roots of this dangerous game can be traced back to ancient times. The legacy of these ancient spies still resonates today, as their techniques and strategies continue to inspire and inform the practices of modern-day intelligence agencies.

In the next chapters, we will explore how the world of espionage evolved throughout history, from the rise of double agents during the Cold War era to the dangerous game of counterintelligence in the modern world. Join us on this thrilling journey as we uncover the hidden lives of double agents and the treacherous world of undercover operations.

Double Agents in the Middle Ages

The Middle Ages, often depicted as a time of knights, castles, and chivalry, also harbored a treacherous world of espionage and double agents. In this subchapter of "Masters of Deceit: Double Agents and the Dangerous Game of Counterintelligence," we delve into the intriguing realm of double agents during this tumultuous period in history.

While the concept of double agents may seem more fitting to the modern era, the Middle Ages witnessed its fair share of double-crossing spies and undercover operatives. In a time rife with political upheaval and power struggles, the need to gather intelligence and manipulate information was as crucial as ever.

From the shadows of medieval courts to the battlefields of warring kingdoms, double agents played a dangerous game, walking a fine line between loyalty and betrayal. They skillfully infiltrated enemy territories, assuming false identities and convincingly aligning themselves with opposing factions. These masters of deceit were able to gain the trust of their enemies, all while secretly reporting back to their true masters.

One intriguing example of a double agent in the Middle Ages is the story of Richard de la Pole, a nobleman who served as a spy for both the French and English during the Hundred Years' War. De la Pole skillfully maneuvered between the two sides, feeding information to both while advancing his own interests. His ability to maintain his cover and deceive his adversaries earned him a fearsome reputation as a master of espionage.

Another notable double agent of the era was John Hawkwood, an English mercenary who switched sides multiple times during the Italian Wars. Hawkwood fought for both the French and the English, often leveraging his knowledge of both sides to gain an advantage. His ability to play both sides of the conflict made him a valuable asset and a formidable opponent.

These tales of medieval double agents highlight the timeless allure of espionage and the dangerous game of counterintelligence. As we explore the lives of these intriguing figures, we uncover the intricate world of double agents throughout history and their role in shaping the events of the Middle Ages.

Whether you are a lover of Cold War espionage stories, historical intrigue, spy thrillers, or political and technological espionage, the stories of double agents in the Middle Ages are sure to captivate your imagination. Join us as we unravel the secrets of these agents, their high-stakes adventures, and the treacherous world of undercover operations they navigated with cunning and guile.

Double Agents in World War I

World War I was a time of great turmoil, not just on the battlefields, but also in the shadowy world of espionage. In the subchapter titled "Double Agents in World War I," we delve into the captivating stories of individuals who played both sides, risking their lives to gather intelligence and deceive their enemies.

During this era, the world witnessed the birth of modern counterintelligence and the dangerous game of double agents. Masters of Deceit: Double Agents and the Dangerous Game of Counterintelligence takes you deep into the intricate web of espionage, revealing the untold stories of these brave men and women who became pawns in the treacherous game of war.

For the public, and particularly those interested in Cold War espionage stories, this subchapter sheds light on the early origins of double agents and their role in shaping the espionage landscape of the 20th century. It explores how these individuals operated in a world where trust was a rare commodity and betrayal was always looming.

Historical espionage enthusiasts will find themselves captivated by the revelations about the lives of double agents throughout history. From Mata Hari's seductive tactics to the cunning maneuvers of Colonel Alexandr Krasnov, these stories take us back in time to witness the birth of modern counterintelligence and the perilous dangers faced by double agents.

The subchapter also appeals to lovers of spy thriller espionage stories, as it uncovers the high-stakes adventures of double agents in the modern world. From secret codes to covert meetings, readers will be transported into a world of intrigue and danger, where every decision could mean life or death.

Furthermore, political espionage enthusiasts will be intrigued by the role of double agents in the realm of international politics. These individuals worked tirelessly to gather vital information that could sway the course of war, often at great personal risk.

As we move into the cyber age, the subchapter also explores the secret lives of double agents in the world of technological espionage. With the rise of cyber warfare, these individuals navigate a complex landscape of virtual threats and digital secrets, a world where a single keystroke can change the course of history.

For those interested in the art of seduction, we delve into the stories of femme fatale double agents who used their charms to manipulate their targets. These women were masters of the subtle game of seduction, using their allure to extract valuable information and carry out their covert missions.

Ultimately, this subchapter sheds light on the dangerous game of counterintelligence and the treacherous world of undercover operations. It delves into the moral complexities faced by double agents, who often found themselves torn between loyalty and duty, forced to make decisions that could have far-reaching consequences.

"Masters of Deceit: Double Agents and the Dangerous Game of Counterintelligence" is a captivating exploration of the world of double agents in World War I. It appeals to a wide range of audiences, from historical enthusiasts to lovers of spy thrillers, and offers a glimpse into a world where trust is a luxury and betrayal is always lurking.

The Rise of Double Agents in World War II

In the tumultuous era of World War II, the world witnessed the rise of a new breed of heroes and villains - double agents. These clandestine operatives played a dangerous game of espionage, navigating treacherous waters to gather critical intelligence and sway the tides of war. Masters of Deceit: Double Agents and the Dangerous Game of Counterintelligence explores their intriguing and often untold stories, captivating readers with tales of bravery, betrayal, and deception.

During the Cold War era, double agents continued to shape the intricate world of espionage. From the ashes of World War II, a new battle emerged - one fought in the shadows. Our book delves into the lives of these enigmatic figures, shedding light on their motivations and the high-stakes adventures they embarked upon. Cold War Espionage Stories provides a thrilling glimpse into the secret lives of double agents, as they played a dangerous game of cat and mouse.

But the history of double agents extends far beyond the Cold War. Throughout history, individuals have walked the treacherous tightrope of double-dealing, risking their lives to gather information and protect their nations. Historical Espionage Stories delves into the lives of these unsung heroes and reveals the untold stories of double agents throughout the ages. From ancient civilizations to the world wars, their impact on shaping the course of history cannot be underestimated.

In the modern world of spy thrillers, double agents continue to captivate our imaginations. Spy Thriller Espionage Stories takes readers on a rollercoaster ride of high-stakes adventures, where the line between good and evil is blurred, and the fate of nations hangs in the balance. Through heart-racing narratives and unexpected twists, readers will discover the thrilling world of double agents in the modern era.

Double agents also find their place in the realm of international politics. Political Espionage Stories uncovers the hidden machinations of double agents in the world of diplomacy and power struggles. From infiltrating enemy governments to manipulating policies, these agents walk a treacherous tightrope, all while balancing their loyalty to their countries and personal ambitions.

As technology advances, so does the world of espionage. Technological Espionage Stories takes readers into the cyber age, where double agents navigate a virtual battlefield. From hacking into secure systems to uncovering state secrets, these agents wield their technical prowess to gather intelligence and change the course of history.

But not all double agents are men. Femme Fatale Espionage Stories explores the art of seduction and the role of women in the dangerous game of espionage. These women use their charm, wit, and intelligence to manipulate and deceive, proving that in the world of double agents, gender knows no bounds.

Espionage Stories: Double Agents and the Dangerous Game of Counterintelligence exposes the thrilling world of double agents, providing a comprehensive look into their treacherous lives. From the ancient world to the cyber age, these agents have shaped the course of history, leaving an indelible mark on the world of espionage.

In Masters of Deceit: Double Agents and the Dangerous Game of Counterintelligence, readers will embark on a captivating journey into the secret lives of these enigmatic figures. Whether you are a lover of history, espionage, or thrilling spy tales, this book is sure to captivate and entertain. Prepare to be enthralled by the dangerous game of counterintelligence and the double agents who mastered it.

Chapter 3: High-Stakes Adventures: Modern Spy Thrillers and Double Agents

The Evolution of Spy Fiction

Subchapter: The Evolution of Spy Fiction

Spy fiction has long captivated readers with its tales of intrigue, danger, and the shadowy world of intelligence operatives. From the early days of the Cold War to the modern era of cyber espionage, the genre has evolved and adapted to reflect the changing times. In this subchapter, we explore the fascinating evolution of spy fiction and its enduring appeal to various niches, including Cold War espionage stories, historical espionage stories, spy thriller espionage stories, political espionage stories, technological espionage stories, femme fatale espionage stories, and the treacherous world of undercover operations.

The Cold War era marked a golden age for spy fiction, where the intricate world of double agents became a focal point. Authors like John le Carré and Ian Fleming crafted stories that delved into the moral ambiguity and complex motivations of spies caught between two superpowers. These stories, filled with suspense and political intrigue, offered a glimpse into the clandestine operations that shaped the era.

Historical espionage stories take readers back in time, unveiling the lives of double agents throughout history. From ancient Rome to World War II, these tales reveal the pivotal roles played by spies in shaping events. Authors such as Robert Harris and Alan Furst meticulously researched historical periods to create gripping narratives that transport readers to a bygone era.

Spy thriller espionage stories bring the genre into the modern world, where high-stakes adventures and technological advancements take center stage. Authors like Daniel Silva and Brad Thor weave tales of espionage that incorporate cutting-edge technology, global conspiracies, and pulse-pounding action. These stories offer a thrilling escape into a world of danger and espionage.

Political espionage stories delve into the realm of international politics, where double agents navigate treacherous waters to serve their countries' interests. Authors like Vince Flynn and Tom Clancy explore the power struggles and covert operations that shape geopolitical events. These stories shed light on the intricate web of alliances, betrayals, and secrets that define the world of political espionage.

Technological espionage stories uncover the secret lives of double agents in the cyber age. With the rise of digital warfare and hacking, authors like Neal Stephenson and William Gibson explore the intersection of technology and espionage. These stories delve into the dark underbelly of the internet, where hackers and spies wage a silent war.

Femme fatale espionage stories focus on the art of seduction and the role of double agents who use their charm and allure to extract information. Authors like John Gardner and Len Deighton create complex female characters who navigate a world of danger and intrigue. These stories challenge traditional gender roles and offer a fresh perspective on the genre.

In the realm of undercover operations, espionage stories shine a light on the dangerous game of counterintelligence. Authors like Robert Ludlum and Frederick Forsyth reveal the sacrifices made by double agents who must maintain their cover while working to uncover threats. These stories explore the psychological toll of living a double life and the constant fear of discovery.

From the Cold War to the cyber age, spy fiction has evolved to reflect the ever-changing world of espionage. Whether delving into historical events or exploring the high-tech world of cyber warfare, these stories continue to captivate readers across various niches. The allure of intrigue, danger, and the unpredictable lives of double agents ensures that spy fiction remains a timeless and enthralling genre.

Real-Life Double Agents in Modern Times

Double agents have long fascinated us with their ability to deceive and manipulate, often working for both sides of a conflict. In this subchapter, we will delve into the intriguing world of real-life double agents in modern times. These individuals, driven by a complex web of motivations, risked their lives to gather intelligence and influence international events.

During the Cold War era, double agents played a pivotal role in shaping the global balance of power. Their stories, filled with intrigue, betrayal, and high-stakes adventures, captivate both history enthusiasts and lovers of spy thrillers. From infamous figures like Kim Philby to less-known heroes like Oleg Gordievsky, we will explore the intricate world of double agents who operated in the shadows.

But the phenomenon of double agents stretches far beyond the Cold War. Throughout history, these individuals have operated in various contexts, driven by different political, personal, and ideological motivations. From ancient civilizations to the present day, the lives of double agents reveal the treacherous nature of undercover operations.

In the modern world, technology has revolutionized espionage, and double agents have adapted to this new reality. The cyber age presents a fertile ground for technological espionage, where double agents navigate the murky waters of hacking, data breaches, and covert information gathering. We will uncover the secret lives of these double agents, shedding light on the ever-evolving nature of espionage in the digital era.

But not all double agents are men. Femme fatales have played a crucial role in the history of espionage. Using their charm, intelligence, and seduction skills, female double agents have influenced the course of international politics. Their stories highlight the delicate dance between love and betrayal, as they manipulate powerful men to extract critical information.

In this subchapter, we will also explore the dangerous game of counterintelligence, where double agents walk a tightrope between discovery and death. Governments and intelligence agencies employ extensive resources to uncover and neutralize these clandestine operatives. We will examine the methods used to catch double agents and the potential consequences they face when exposed.

Whether you are fascinated by the historical context, the thrilling adventures, the political implications, or the technological aspects, the world of double agents offers a captivating narrative. Join us as we uncover the lives and stories of real-life double agents, shining a light on the dangerous game of counterintelligence and the treacherous world of undercover operations.

The Dangers and Challenges of Being a Double Agent

In the realm of espionage, few roles are as perilous and complex as that of a double agent. Double agents, also known as moles or spies, operate within the shadows, straddling the thin line between loyalty and betrayal. These masters of deceit play a dangerous game of counterintelligence, risking their lives to gather vital information for their handlers while simultaneously deceiving their enemies.

For those captivated by the intricate world of double agents during the Cold War era, the dangers and challenges they faced were unparalleled. The stakes were high, with global superpowers locked in a battle for dominance. Double agents became pawns in a vast chess game, where a single wrong move could lead to exposure, capture, or even death. The constant fear of being discovered, always looking over their shoulders, took a toll on their mental and emotional well-being.

Unveiling the lives of double agents throughout history reveals a pattern of treachery and bravery. From ancient times to the modern era, these individuals walked a tightrope of deceit, navigating the murky waters of political espionage. They faced the constant threat of isolation, betrayal from within their own ranks, and the moral dilemma of balancing their loyalty to their country with their loyalty to their handlers.

In the realm of spy thriller espionage stories, the adventures of double agents in the modern world continue to captivate readers and viewers alike. High-stakes missions, heart-pounding chases, and deadly encounters are the norm for these brave souls. Their ability to blend seamlessly into different cultures, assuming false identities, is a testament to their training and resilience.

Double agents in the realm of international politics navigate a treacherous world where loyalties are constantly tested. They must carefully choose sides, playing both friend and foe, all while ensuring their true intentions remain hidden. The delicate balance of power in the geopolitical landscape makes their role all the more dangerous, as the consequences of their actions can have far-reaching implications.

The rise of the cyber age has given birth to a new breed of double agents. In the world of technological espionage, these individuals operate in the digital realm, stealing classified information, sabotaging systems, and manipulating data. Their secret lives unfold behind a screen, as they employ their technical expertise to gain access to sensitive information.

The art of seduction and the femme fatale play a significant role in the lives of double agents. These masters of manipulation use their charm, wit, and beauty to extract information from their targets. They understand the power of allure and how it can be used to their advantage, making them formidable adversaries in the dangerous game of counterintelligence.

In the treacherous world of undercover operations, double agents are the unsung heroes. Their willingness to sacrifice their own safety for the greater good is a testament to their courage and dedication. They live in constant danger, always aware that their next mission could be their last.

The dangers and challenges faced by double agents are as diverse as the niches of espionage stories. From the intricacies of Cold War espionage to the high-stakes adventures of modern-day spies, these individuals navigate a perilous path, forever marked by secrecy, danger, and the constant threat of betrayal.

The Impact of Double Agents on Global Security

In the realm of espionage and counterintelligence, few figures are as intriguing and dangerous as double agents. These individuals, who operate undercover as spies for one side while secretly working for another, have the power to shape the course of history and significantly impact global security. In "Masters of Deceit: Double Agents and the Dangerous Game of Counterintelligence," we delve into the complex world of double agents and explore their profound influence on the international stage.

During the Cold War era, the intricate web of double agents played a pivotal role in shaping the balance of power between the United States and the Soviet Union. These agents, often driven by ideology, personal gain, or a mixture of both, infiltrated the highest levels of government and intelligence agencies. Their actions had far-reaching consequences, impacting not only diplomatic relations but also military strategies and technological advancements.

Throughout history, double agents have existed in various forms, transcending time and borders. From ancient civilizations to modern times, their stories have captivated audiences seeking thrilling tales of espionage and intrigue. By unveiling the lives of these double agents, we gain a deeper understanding of the motivations that drive individuals to betray their own countries and the lasting impact they have on the world.

In the realm of spy thrillers, double agents are the ultimate protagonists. Their high-stakes adventures, filled with danger and suspense, keep readers on the edge of their seats. From daring escapes to intricate plots, these stories showcase the cunning and resourcefulness required to navigate the treacherous world of espionage.

Double agents also play a significant role in the realm of international politics. Their actions can influence the outcome of elections, shape public opinion, and even determine the fate of nations. In an increasingly interconnected world, where information is power, the actions of double agents can have far-reaching consequences on political stability and global security.

With the advent of the digital age, double agents have also adapted to the new landscape of technological espionage. Operating in the shadows of cyberspace, these agents utilize their knowledge of technology to gather intelligence, disrupt enemy operations, and manipulate information. The secret lives of these double agents in the cyber age reveal the ever-evolving nature of the dangerous game of counterintelligence.

In this book, we also explore the art of seduction employed by femme fatale double agents. These skilled operatives use their charm, beauty, and charisma to extract valuable information and manipulate their targets. Their stories shed light on the power dynamics at play in the world of espionage and the complex relationships that form between double agents and their handlers.

Ultimately, "Masters of Deceit: Double Agents and the Dangerous Game of Counterintelligence" unveils the intricate world of double agents and their profound impact on global security. By delving into their stories, we gain a deeper appreciation for the dangerous game they play and the ever-present threat they pose to the delicate balance of power in the world.

Chapter 4: Double Agents in the Realm of International Politics

The Interplay Between Espionage and Politics

In the realm of international politics, a dangerous game of deception and intrigue has been played out for centuries. This game is espionage, and at the heart of it lies the complex interplay between espionage and politics. In the book "Masters of Deceit: Double Agents and the Dangerous Game of Counterintelligence," we delve into the captivating world of double agents and their crucial role in shaping the course of history.

During the Cold War era, espionage reached unprecedented heights. The world was divided into two superpowers, the United States and the Soviet Union, locked in a constant struggle for supremacy. Both sides sought to gain an edge through covert operations and intelligence gathering, employing double agents to infiltrate enemy ranks, gather classified information, and mislead their adversaries.

These double agents were masters of deception, skilled in the art of playing both sides. They operated in the shadows, navigating treacherous waters where trust was a rare commodity. Their actions had far-reaching consequences, influencing political decisions, shaping foreign policies, and even altering the outcome of wars.

Throughout history, double agents have played pivotal roles in shaping the destiny of nations. From the infamous Mata Hari during World War I to the enigmatic Kim Philby during the Cold War, their stories are a testament to the power and danger of espionage. These historical espionage stories provide a unique window into the lives of these clandestine operatives, offering insight into their motivations, their methods, and the sacrifices they made in service to their countries.

In the modern world, the game of espionage has evolved. Technology has become a powerful weapon in the hands of double agents, enabling them to operate in the cyber realm. Technological espionage stories bring to light the secret lives of these agents, showcasing their skills in hacking, code-breaking, and manipulating digital information.

But espionage is not limited to the realm of technology and politics. It is a world where seduction and manipulation go hand in hand. Femme fatale espionage stories explore the art of seduction employed by double agents, highlighting their ability to exploit vulnerabilities, manipulate emotions, and extract sensitive information.

In this book, we take you on a thrilling journey through the dangerous game of counterintelligence. We delve into the treacherous world of undercover operations, where double agents risk their lives to protect their countries and achieve their objectives. Espionage stories are not just tales of intrigue and adventure; they are a reflection of the complex web of power, politics, and deception that defines our world.

For those fascinated by the intricacies of the Cold War era, historical espionage stories offer a glimpse into a time when the world teetered on the brink of nuclear war. For lovers of spy thrillers, these stories provide high-stakes adventures filled with suspense, danger, and unexpected twists. And for those interested in the world of politics, the interplay between espionage and politics reveals the hidden forces that shape the course of history.

Join us as we uncover the fascinating lives of double agents, explore the treacherous world of espionage, and unravel the intricate web of power and deception. "Masters of Deceit: Double Agents and the Dangerous Game of Counterintelligence" is a captivating journey into a world where nothing is as it seems, and the stakes could not be higher.

Double Agents in Diplomatic Circles

In the riveting subchapter titled "Double Agents in Diplomatic Circles" from the book "Masters of Deceit: Double Agents and the Dangerous Game of Counterintelligence," we delve into the intriguing world of espionage during the Cold War era and beyond. This chapter will captivate readers from all walks of life, including Cold War espionage enthusiasts, history buffs, spy thriller lovers, political aficionados, technology enthusiasts, and those fascinated by the art of seduction and the treacherous world of undercover operations.

Throughout history, double agents have played a pivotal role in shaping the geopolitical landscape, and this subchapter sheds light on their covert activities within diplomatic circles. It unravels the complex web of deceit, betrayal, and high-stakes adventures that these double agents engage in to protect their countries' interests or fulfill their personal agendas.

Readers will be transported back to the heart of the Cold War, where the world stood divided between the East and the West. They will discover the intricate lives of double agents who seamlessly operated within diplomatic circles, using their access to classified information to manipulate events, sow discord, and further their clandestine missions.

Moreover, this subchapter explores the historical significance of double agents throughout the ages. From ancient times to modern-day cyber espionage, these enigmatic individuals have shaped the course of history, often remaining hidden in the shadows, their true identities known only to a select few.

The subchapter also delves into the thrilling world of spy thrillers, where double agents become the focal point of high-stakes adventures. Drawing inspiration from real-life events, readers will be enthralled by the heart-pounding narratives that unfold as double agents navigate treacherous waters, battling against time and the ever-looming threat of exposure.

Additionally, this subchapter explores the intersection of politics and espionage, highlighting the role of double agents in the realm of international politics. From infiltrating foreign governments to influencing policy decisions, these covert operatives wield immense power and pose a constant threat to the delicate balance of power.

Finally, readers will be introduced to the evolving landscape of technological espionage. In the cyber age, double agents harness the power of technology to breach digital fortresses, steal classified information, and wreak havoc on a global scale. This subchapter sheds light on the secret lives of these modern-day double agents and the growing importance of cybersecurity in an interconnected world.

In conclusion, "Double Agents in Diplomatic Circles" provides a captivating journey through the dangerous game of counterintelligence. Regardless of their particular interests, readers will find themselves engrossed in the riveting stories of double agents, their art of seduction, and the treacherous world of undercover operations.

The Manipulative Nature of Political Espionage

Title: The Manipulative Nature of Political Espionage: Unveiling the Intricate World of Double Agents

Introduction:

In the realm of international politics, where power and influence are constantly at stake, a dangerous game of counterintelligence has been played for centuries. From the Cold War era to the modern cyber age, double agents have played a pivotal role in shaping history and altering the course of nations. This subchapter delves into the manipulative nature of political espionage, exploring the intricate world of double agents and their treacherous undercover operations.

Understanding the Double Agent:

Double agents, the masters of deceit, operate in the shadows, skillfully manipulating their way into the confidence of both sides. They infiltrate intelligence agencies, governments, and even the highest echelons of power, exploiting vulnerabilities and gathering sensitive information. These agents are the embodiment of duplicity, capable of switching allegiances at a moment's notice to serve their own interests or those of their handlers.

The Art of Manipulation:

Political espionage relies heavily on the art of manipulation. Double agents possess a unique ability to exploit human weaknesses, whether it be greed, ambition, or ideological fervor. They understand the intricacies of power dynamics and use this knowledge to their advantage, pitting adversaries against each other or creating chaos within enemy ranks. Through deception, they gain access to classified information, feeding their handlers with vital intelligence.

The High-Stakes Adventures:

The dangerous world of political espionage is fraught with high-stakes adventures. Double agents risk exposure, betrayal, and even their lives, as they navigate the treacherous waters of international politics. Their actions have the power to ignite wars, topple governments, or expose hidden agendas. Whether it's the tense standoffs of the Cold War, or the modern-day cyber espionage battles, the stakes are always at their peak.

The Femme Fatale Factor:

The art of seduction plays a crucial role in political espionage, with femme fatale double agents employing their charm and allure to manipulate their targets. These seductive spies use their beauty and charisma to extract valuable information, compromise key individuals, and even influence critical decision-making processes. Their role in the world of espionage is both fascinating and dangerous, as they navigate a fine line between loyalty and personal gain.

Conclusion:

Political espionage is a dangerous game, where the manipulative nature of double agents takes center stage. From the Cold War era to the cyber age, these masters of deceit have shaped the course of history, leaving an indelible mark on the world of international politics. Their ability to manipulate, exploit, and deceive continues to captivate audiences, making political espionage stories a thrilling and intriguing genre for the public. Through their treacherous undercover operations, double agents remind us of the complex and intricate nature of the human psyche, and the lengths individuals will go to achieve their objectives.

Case Studies of Double Agents in High-Level Politics

In the shadowy world of espionage, few figures are as intriguing and enigmatic as the double agent. These individuals, who operate as trusted insiders while secretly working for another nation or organization, have played a pivotal role in shaping the course of history. In this subchapter, we delve into the captivating stories of double agents who infiltrated high-level politics, leaving an indelible mark on the world stage.

During the Cold War era, double agents became a crucial tool in the battle between East and West. One such case is that of Kim Philby, a British intelligence officer who rose through the ranks of MI6 while secretly spying for the Soviet Union. His betrayal not only compromised countless operations but also had far-reaching geopolitical consequences. Philby's story offers a glimpse into the intricate world of double agents during this tense period.

Moving beyond the Cold War, historical espionage stories provide us with a broader perspective on the lives of double agents throughout history. We explore the exploits of Mata Hari, the infamous femme fatale who used her seductive charms to extract information during World War I. Her story illustrates the timeless allure of double agents and the dangers they face in a treacherous world of undercover operations.

In the modern world, political espionage continues to shape international relations. The case of Aldrich Ames, a CIA officer turned double agent for the Soviet Union, highlights the high-stakes adventures that unfold in this realm. Ames' actions resulted in the exposure and execution of numerous American assets, leaving a trail of devastation in his wake.

Technological advancements have also given rise to a new breed of double agents in the cyber age. We explore the secret lives of individuals like Edward Snowden, who used their access to classified information to expose government surveillance programs. These cases shed light on the complex intersection of technology, espionage, and the dangerous game of counterintelligence.

Whether it is the allure of seduction or the thirst for power, double agents continue to captivate our imagination. From the pages of Cold War espionage stories to the thrilling world of spy thrillers, these individuals have left an indelible mark on history. Join us as we uncover their stories and unravel the intricate web of deception that has shaped the world we live in.

Chapter 5: The Cyber Age: Technological Espionage and Double Agents

The Emergence of Cyber Espionage

Title: The Emergence of Cyber Espionage: Unveiling the Secret Lives of Double Agents in the Cyber Age

Introduction:

In the ever-evolving world of espionage, the emergence of cyber espionage has revolutionized the dangerous game of counterintelligence. In this subchapter, we delve into the intricate world of double agents and their high-stakes adventures in the modern cyber age. From the Cold War era to the present day, the lives of these double agents have been shaped by political agendas, technological advancements, international politics, and the treacherous world of undercover operations. Join us as we explore the secret lives of double agents and their role in the realm of cyber espionage.

Body:

1. The Cold War Era: Espionage in a Divided World

During the Cold War, the world witnessed a rise in double agents who played crucial roles in gathering classified information. From the Cambridge Five to Aldrich Ames, we uncover the stories of these double agents who infiltrated the intelligence agencies of their respective countries, leaving a lasting impact on the world of counterintelligence.

2. The Technological Revolution: Espionage Enters the Cyber Age

With the advent of the internet and rapid technological advancements, espionage found a new battleground in cyberspace. Double agents skilled in hacking and cyber warfare became valuable assets to nations seeking to gain an edge over their adversaries. We explore the exploits of these tech-savvy spies and their role in shaping the cyber landscape.

3. Political Espionage: The Double Agent's Role in International Politics

In the realm of international politics, double agents have played a pivotal role in shaping the course of history. We uncover the stories of spies who infiltrated governments, political organizations, and influential circles, gathering valuable intelligence to advance their nation's interests.

4. Femme Fatale Espionage: The Art of Seduction in the Spy World

The world of espionage is not without its femme fatales. Double agents, often skilled in the art of seduction, have used their charm and allure to extract classified information from their targets. We explore the dangerous game of double agents who have mastered the art of seduction, often risking their own lives in the process.

Conclusion:

From the Cold War era to the present day, the dangerous game of counterintelligence has witnessed the emergence of cyber espionage. Double agents, operating in the realms of international politics, technology, and undercover operations, have shaped the course of history. Their stories of high-stakes adventures, treachery, and deception continue to captivate audiences interested in Cold War espionage, historical intrigue, spy thrillers, and the ever-evolving world of cyber espionage.

The Secret Lives of Double Agents in the Digital Realm

In the world of espionage, double agents have always played a pivotal role. These individuals, who operate undercover within enemy organizations, possess the unique ability to gather critical intelligence and manipulate events from within. While the concept of a double agent may seem like something out of a thrilling spy novel, the reality is that these covert operatives have existed throughout history, and continue to infiltrate the deepest realms of international politics and technological espionage.

During the Cold War era, double agents became prominent figures, navigating the intricate world of espionage with finesse and cunning. In "Masters of Deceit: Double Agents and the Dangerous Game of Counterintelligence," we delve into the lives of these enigmatic individuals, exploring their motivations, methods, and the treacherous world of undercover operations they inhabit.

Unveiling the lives of double agents throughout history, we shed light on the dangerous game they play, where trust is scarce and betrayal is a constant threat. With gripping accounts of their high-stakes adventures, we bring to life the thrilling world of political espionage, where every move can mean the difference between life and death.

In the modern world, the digital realm has become a breeding ground for espionage. The rise of technology has opened up new avenues for double agents to operate, and the cyber age has become their playground. Through our exploration of technological espionage stories, we reveal the secret lives of these double agents, who skillfully navigate the complex world of hacking, data breaches, and cyber warfare.

But it is not just the realm of technology that double agents exploit. The art of seduction also plays a crucial role in their operations. In femme fatale espionage stories, we delve into the world of double agents and the art of seduction. These individuals use their charm, wit, and beauty to manipulate targets and extract information, leaving a trail of broken hearts and shattered lives in their wake.

Espionage is a dangerous game, and double agents are at the heart of it all. In this subchapter of "Masters of Deceit: Double Agents and the Dangerous Game of Counterintelligence," we bring you stories that will captivate and thrill. Whether you are a fan of cold war espionage stories, historical espionage tales, spy thriller adventures, or the treacherous world of international politics, this book has something for everyone.

Join us as we unveil the secret lives of double agents, and explore the dangerous game of counterintelligence they play. Let the thrilling world of espionage captivate your imagination, as we delve into the treacherous world of undercover operations. Get ready for a heart-pounding journey into the unknown, where trust is scarce, and danger lurks in every shadow.

The Role of Double Agents in Cyber Warfare

In the ever-evolving world of espionage, double agents have always played a crucial role. These individuals, who work undercover for one intelligence agency while secretly providing information to another, have been instrumental in shaping the course of history. From the Cold War era to the modern age of cyber warfare, double agents have been at the forefront of covert operations and clandestine activities.

During the Cold War, double agents were an integral part of the intricate world of espionage. These brave individuals infiltrated enemy organizations, risking their lives to gather valuable intelligence. Their actions helped shape the geopolitical landscape and prevented catastrophic events. The stories of these double agents, such as Kim Philby and Aldrich Ames, continue to captivate audiences intrigued by the dangerous world of Cold War espionage.

But the role of double agents didn't end with the Cold War. In fact, it has become even more important in the age of cyber warfare. With the advent of the internet and advanced technologies, espionage has taken a new form. Double agents are now operating in the digital realm, infiltrating enemy networks and stealing valuable information. These technological espionage stories, with their high-stakes adventures and the treacherous world of undercover operations, have become the stuff of spy thriller novels and movies.

Double agents in the realm of international politics also play a significant role. These individuals infiltrate political organizations, gaining the trust of influential figures, and providing valuable information to intelligence agencies. Their actions have the power to shape the policies of nations and impact global affairs. The dangerous game of counterintelligence, where double agents walk a tightrope between loyalty and betrayal, keeps readers and viewers on the edge of their seats.

In the cyber age, double agents have become even more elusive and dangerous. Operating in the world of technological espionage, they navigate the complex web of digital networks, using their skills to manipulate and deceive. The secret lives of these double agents involve the use of cutting-edge technology, as they exploit vulnerabilities in computer systems and gather intelligence from the shadows.

Double agents have also mastered the art of seduction, with femme fatales playing a prominent role in espionage stories. These seductive spies use their charm and beauty to extract information from their targets, often leading to deadly consequences. Their stories are filled with intrigue, danger, and the ultimate betrayal.

Whether in the Cold War era or the modern age of cyber warfare, double agents continue to hold a prominent place in the world of espionage. Their actions shape the course of history, and their stories captivate audiences across various niches. From historical espionage stories to spy thriller adventures, the dangerous game of counterintelligence remains a subject of fascination for the public.

The Ethical Dilemmas of Technological Espionage

In today's interconnected world, where technology dominates every aspect of our lives, the realm of espionage has evolved. Gone are the days of trench coats and hidden microfilm; now, the battleground lies in the cyber domain. Technological espionage, a term coined to describe the covert activities of double agents in the cyber age, presents a myriad of ethical dilemmas that demand our attention.

For the public, it is essential to understand the implications of technological espionage. Cold War Espionage Stories: The Intricate World of Double Agents during the Cold War Era, Historical Espionage Stories: Unveiling the Lives of Double Agents Throughout History, and Spy Thriller Espionage Stories: High-Stakes Adventures of Double Agents in the Modern World, will find this subchapter particularly intriguing. It sheds light on the shadowy world of double agents in the cyber age, revealing their methods, motives, and the dangerous game they play.

One of the key ethical dilemmas in technological espionage is the violation of privacy. Double agents infiltrate networks, breach firewalls, and hack into secure databases, all in the name of gathering intelligence. But at what cost? This subchapter explores the moral implications of invading individuals' privacy, the potential for abuse, and the erosion of trust in the digital era.

For those fascinated by Political Espionage Stories: Double Agents in the Realm of International Politics, Technological Espionage Stories: The Secret Lives of Double Agents in the Cyber Age, and Femme Fatale Espionage Stories: Double Agents and the Art of Seduction, this subchapter delves into the complexities of the double agent's role. It examines the delicate balance between loyalty and betrayal, the manipulation of trust, and the dangerous allure of power that often entices these agents to walk the treacherous path of espionage.

Furthermore, this subchapter addresses the broader implications of technological espionage. Espionage Stories: Double Agents and the Dangerous Game of Counterintelligence, and Espionage Stories: Double Agents and the Treacherous World of Undercover Operations, will resonate with readers seeking to understand the intricate web of counterintelligence operations. It explores the potential consequences of technological espionage, such as the escalation of cyber warfare, the destabilization of nations, and the erosion of democracy.

In conclusion, The Ethical Dilemmas of Technological Espionage is a subchapter that appeals to a diverse range of readership. It uncovers the hidden world of double agents in the cyber age, providing insights into the moral quandaries they face. Whether you are interested in historical espionage, political intrigue, or the treacherous world of undercover operations, this subchapter offers a thought-provoking exploration of the ethical dilemmas that permeate the realm of technological espionage.

Chapter 6: Double Agents and the Art of Seduction: Femme Fatales in Espionage

The Seductive Power of Double Agents

In the world of espionage, few figures captivate our imagination quite like the double agent. These elusive individuals possess a unique ability to navigate the treacherous waters of counterintelligence, playing both sides to their advantage. Masters of Deceit: Double Agents and the Dangerous Game of Counterintelligence delves deep into the intricate lives of these enigmatic characters, exploring their motivations, methods, and the seductive power they wielded.

From the Cold War era to the modern world of cyber espionage, double agents have left an indelible mark on history. Their stories are not only enthralling, but they also offer valuable insights into the complex realm of international politics. As we plunge into the pages of this book, we are transported into a world where loyalty is a fragile concept and trust is a luxury few can afford.

One cannot discuss double agents without unraveling the captivating web of their relationships. These individuals possess an uncanny ability to exploit the vulnerabilities of others, using charm, seduction, and manipulation as their weapons. The femme fatale double agent, in particular, weaves a captivating tale of danger and seduction, using her wits and allure to extract valuable information from unsuspecting targets.

The dangerous game of counterintelligence is not confined to the physical realm alone. In the cyber age, the battlefield has expanded, and technological espionage has taken center stage. Double agents operating in this domain possess an intimate understanding of the intricacies of digital warfare, leveraging their skills to infiltrate sensitive systems and steal coveted information.

Through the pages of Masters of Deceit, we embark on a thrilling journey that unveils the lives of double agents throughout history. From the grand-scale geopolitical landscape to the clandestine world of undercover operations, their stories offer a unique perspective on the shadowy realm of espionage.

Whether you are a history enthusiast, a lover of spy thrillers, or simply intrigued by the dangerous game of counterintelligence, this subchapter will transport you into a world where loyalties are tested, and deception reigns supreme. Brace yourself for high-stakes adventures, heart-pounding suspense, and a glimpse into the seductive power of double agents.

Famous Female Double Agents in History

Throughout history, the world of espionage has been predominantly associated with men. However, behind the scenes, there were remarkable women who played a crucial role as double agents, infiltrating enemy lines and gathering invaluable intelligence. In this subchapter, we explore the lives of some of the most famous female double agents in history, shedding light on their incredible stories and their contributions to the dangerous game of counterintelligence.

One such notable figure is Mata Hari, the infamous Dutch exotic dancer turned spy during World War I. Known for her beauty and charm, Mata Hari utilized her seductive persona to extract critical information from high-ranking officials and military officers. However, her double life came to a tragic end when she was executed for espionage in 1917.

Another remarkable double agent was Odette Sansom, a British-French spy during World War II. Sansom, along with her husband, operated as part of the Special Operations Executive (SOE) and undertook daring missions in Nazi-occupied France. Despite enduring torture and imprisonment, Sansom never revealed any information to her captors, and she was eventually awarded the George Cross for her bravery.

In the realm of Cold War espionage, one cannot overlook the contributions of Christine Granville, a Polish-British spy who worked for the British Special Operations Executive. Granville's accomplishments included infiltrating Nazi-occupied Poland and assisting in the rescue of British prisoners of war. Her courage and resourcefulness earned her numerous commendations and made her one of the most celebrated operatives of her time.

Moving into the modern era, we encounter the story of Anna Chapman, a Russian spy who operated in the United States in the early 2010s. Chapman, along with other members of the "Illegals Program," was apprehended by the FBI in a high-profile case that exposed a network of Russian espionage. Chapman's glamorous image and her use of technology to communicate with her handlers made her a symbol of the evolving world of double agents.

These women, along with many others, exemplify the complex and treacherous world of double agents. Their stories not only captivate our imagination but also remind us of the significant contributions made by women in the field of espionage. As we delve into the lives of these famous female double agents, we gain a deeper understanding of the challenges they faced, the risks they took, and the secrets they uncovered, ultimately shaping the course of history.

Whether you are drawn to the intrigue of Cold War espionage, fascinated by historical undercover operations, or seeking high-stakes adventures in spy thriller stories, the tales of these remarkable women will leave you inspired and eager to explore the multifaceted world of double agents. So buckle up for a thrilling journey as we uncover the secret lives of famous female double agents and their invaluable contributions to the dangerous game of counterintelligence.

The Psychological Manipulation of Femme Fatales

Subchapter: The Psychological Manipulation of Femme Fatales

In the world of espionage, double agents have always played a crucial role in gathering information and turning the tide of international conflicts. Among these covert operatives, the femme fatales have emerged as intriguing characters, using their beauty, charm, and seduction skills to manipulate their targets. This subchapter delves into the psychological manipulation tactics employed by these seductive spies and their impact on the dangerous game of counterintelligence.

During the Cold War era, the intricate world of double agents witnessed the rise of femme fatales who operated at the intersection of political espionage, historical intrigues, and high-stakes adventures. Masters of deceit, these women mastered the art of psychological manipulation, exploiting the vulnerabilities and desires of their targets to extract valuable information. Their ability to create illusions of intimacy and trust made them formidable assets in the realm of international politics.

Drawing from historical espionage stories, we unveil the lives of these double agents throughout history. From Mata Hari, the notorious World War I spy, to modern-day undercover operatives, their stories shed light on the complex dynamics of the spy world. The psychological manipulation techniques employed by these femme fatales will leave readers captivated, as they uncover the secrets behind their successful double lives.

Spy thriller enthusiasts will be particularly drawn to the high-stakes adventures of these covert operatives in the modern world. This subchapter reveals the dangerous game of cat and mouse, where the lines between friend and foe blur. With political espionage as the backdrop, readers will be enthralled by the treacherous world these double agents navigate, risking their lives for the sake of national security.

In the cyber age, technological espionage has become increasingly prevalent. Uncovering the secret lives of femme fatales operating in this realm gives readers a glimpse into the ever-evolving tactics employed by double agents. From hacking to social engineering, their manipulation skills extend beyond physical interactions, making them formidable adversaries in the world of counterintelligence.

For those fascinated by the art of seduction, this subchapter explores how femme fatales employ their charm to manipulate targets. Their ability to exploit desires and weaknesses, while maintaining an air of mystery, is a testament to the power of psychological manipulation. With a focus on the dangerous game of espionage, readers will be enthralled by the stories of these seductive spies and the impact they have had on the world stage.

In conclusion, this subchapter uncovers the psychological manipulation tactics employed by femme fatales in the realm of espionage. From historical intrigues to modern-day adventures, these double agents use their charm and seduction skills to extract valuable information. With a focus on the dangerous game of counterintelligence, readers from various niches will be captivated by the complex lives of these seductive spies.

The Consequences of Betrayal in Love and Espionage

Chapter 7: The Consequences of Betrayal in Love and Espionage

In the intricate world of espionage, where loyalty is a rarity and trust is a luxury, the consequences of betrayal are both devastating and far-reaching. This subchapter explores the dangerous game of double agents and the harrowing aftermath of their actions in the realm of love and espionage.

During the Cold War era, double agents played a pivotal role in the high-stakes world of espionage. They operated in the shadows, balancing on the thin line between loyalty and treachery. These individuals were masters of deceit, seamlessly navigating the complexities of international politics while maintaining multiple identities. However, when the facade crumbled and their true intentions were unveiled, the consequences were dire.

Betrayal in love and espionage carries a heavy toll, not only for the individuals directly involved but also for the nations they served. The exposure of a double agent not only compromises national security but also erodes public trust in intelligence agencies. The impact reverberates through the political landscape, causing ripples that can destabilize entire governments.

Historical espionage stories are replete with tales of double agents whose actions altered the course of history. Their betrayal led to the downfall of empires, the unraveling of secret alliances, and the loss of countless lives. From the infamous Cambridge Spy Ring to the enigmatic figure of Kim Philby, these stories serve as cautionary tales, reminding us of the consequences of placing too much trust in those who walk a dangerous path.

In the modern world, the stakes have only grown higher. Technological espionage stories shed light on the secret lives of double agents in the cyber age. These individuals navigate a treacherous landscape where a single keystroke can bring down nations. The consequences of their betrayal extend beyond physical borders, impacting the global economy, infrastructure, and the lives of everyday citizens.

Femme fatales have long been a staple of spy thrillers, but their role in espionage goes beyond mere seduction. The art of manipulation intertwines with the treacherous world of undercover operations, blurring the lines between love and espionage. These double agents wield their charm as a weapon, ensnaring their targets in a web of deceit. But when the facade crumbles, the consequences can be devastating for all those involved.

In conclusion, the consequences of betrayal in love and espionage are far-reaching and profound. From the Cold War era to the cyber age, the stories of double agents serve as cautionary tales, reminding us of the dangers inherent in the treacherous world of counterintelligence. Whether driven by ideology, greed, or a thirst for power, the consequences of their actions reverberate through history, altering the course of nations and leaving a trail of destruction in their wake.

Chapter 7: The Dangerous Game of Counterintelligence: Unmasking Double Agents

The Cat and Mouse of Counterintelligence

"The Cat and Mouse of Counterintelligence"

In the thrilling world of espionage, the game of counterintelligence is like a never-ending cat and mouse chase. In this subchapter, we delve into the intricacies and dangers of this dangerous game, exploring the lives of double agents who operated during the Cold War era and beyond. Masters of Deceit: Double Agents and the Dangerous Game of Counterintelligence takes you on a captivating journey through the shadowy world of spies, revealing the high-stakes adventures, treacherous missions, and the constant battle for survival.

During the Cold War, double agents played a pivotal role in shaping history. They were individuals who operated on both sides of the iron curtain, walking a dangerous tightrope between loyalty and betrayal. These brave men and women risked their lives in the pursuit of gathering intelligence, often living double lives filled with secrecy and deception. From the infamous Cambridge Five to the lesser-known figures, this subchapter unveils the lives of these double agents and their impact on international politics.

But the cat and mouse game didn't end with the Cold War. In the modern world, the game of counterintelligence has evolved, incorporating new technologies and threats. The rise of cyber espionage has given birth to a new breed of double agents who operate in the digital realm. The technological espionage stories in this subchapter shed light on the secret lives of these agents, their methods, and the ever-present danger they face.

Espionage is not just about men; women have also played a significant role in this dangerous game. Femme fatales, skilled in the art of seduction, have used their charm and wits to extract crucial information from unsuspecting targets. This subchapter explores the captivating stories of female double agents, highlighting their roles in shaping history and their unique contributions to the world of espionage.

Through captivating storytelling and meticulous research, Masters of Deceit: Double Agents and the Dangerous Game of Counterintelligence offers an immersive experience. It appeals to a wide range of audiences, including those interested in cold war espionage stories, historical espionage stories, spy thriller espionage stories, political espionage stories, technological espionage stories, femme fatale espionage stories, and anyone intrigued by the treacherous world of undercover operations.

Prepare to be captivated by the dangerous game of counterintelligence, as we explore the lives of double agents who risked it all for their countries and the shadows they inhabited. Masters of Deceit offers a unique glimpse into the secret world of spies, leaving readers on the edge of their seats, eager to uncover the next thrilling twist in this cat and mouse chase.

Techniques and Strategies Used in Uncovering Double Agents

In the thrilling realm of espionage and counterintelligence, the game of uncovering double agents is a dangerous and intricate one. Masters of Deceit: Double Agents and the Dangerous Game of Counterintelligence explores the captivating stories of double agents throughout history, from the Cold War era to the modern world. This subchapter delves into the techniques and strategies employed by intelligence agencies to expose these treacherous individuals operating within their ranks.

During the Cold War, the stakes were high, and the world was divided into two ideological camps. In this era, intelligence agencies developed a range of strategies to identify and neutralize double agents. One such technique was the use of intelligence tradecraft, which involved the meticulous analysis of information, surveillance, and the recruitment of informants within the intelligence community. By carefully studying patterns, inconsistencies, and behaviors, counterintelligence agents were able to piece together the puzzle and uncover the secret identities of these deceitful individuals.

The advent of technology in the modern age has brought about a whole new set of challenges and opportunities for double agents. With the rise of cyber espionage, intelligence agencies have had to adapt their techniques to the digital realm. The use of advanced data analytics, artificial intelligence, and machine learning has become crucial in identifying patterns and anomalies that could potentially expose a double agent. The book explores how agencies have embraced these technological advancements to stay one step ahead in the dangerous game of counterintelligence.

In addition to technological advancements, the art of seduction has also played a significant role in the world of double agents. Femme fatales have long been used to lure unsuspecting individuals into revealing sensitive information or becoming unwitting pawns in a larger game. The book delves into the tactics employed by double agents skilled in the art of seduction, and how intelligence agencies have worked to uncover their true motives.

Uncovering double agents is a treacherous and delicate task, and the stakes are always high. The stories shared in this subchapter will captivate readers with their tales of high-stakes adventures, treacherous undercover operations, and the dangerous game of counterintelligence. Whether you are a history enthusiast, a fan of spy thrillers, or simply intrigued by the intricate world of espionage, Masters of Deceit will take you on a thrilling journey through the lives of double agents and the strategies employed to expose them.

The Role of Double Agents in Counterintelligence Operations

Introduction:

In the intricate world of espionage, double agents play a pivotal role in the dangerous game of counterintelligence. These individuals, often living double lives, infiltrate enemy organizations or intelligence agencies and provide valuable information to their handlers. "Masters of Deceit: Double Agents and the Dangerous Game of Counterintelligence" delves into the captivating stories of these double agents throughout history, exploring their role in various niches, from Cold War espionage to the treacherous world of undercover operations. This subchapter, addressed to the public and tailored to multiple niches, aims to shed light on the crucial role double agents have played in counterintelligence operations.

The Role of Double Agents:

Double agents are a unique breed of spies who operate on both sides of the fence. They gain the trust of their adversaries while secretly working for their own intelligence agencies. Their primary objective is to gather classified information, disrupt enemy operations, and mislead their opponents. These individuals possess exceptional acting skills, adaptability, and a deep understanding of the enemy's mindset.

Cold War Espionage Stories:

During the Cold War era, double agents played a vital role in shaping the geopolitical landscape. They infiltrated the highest levels of enemy intelligence agencies, providing crucial information that influenced decision-making and prevented potential conflicts. Their stories are filled with suspense, tension, and high-stakes adventures.

Historical Espionage Stories:

Unveiling the Lives of Double Agents Throughout History:

Double agents have existed throughout history, from ancient civilizations to modern times. This subchapter explores the lives of double agents who operated in different eras, shedding light on their motivations, successes, and failures. Their stories reveal the timeless allure and danger of espionage.

Spy Thriller Espionage Stories:

High-Stakes Adventures of Double Agents in the Modern World:

In the modern world, double agents face new challenges brought on by advances in technology and the ever-evolving nature of global politics. This subchapter delves into the thrilling world of modern espionage, where double agents navigate the intricate web of cyber intelligence, political intrigue, and high-stakes missions.

Political Espionage Stories:

Double Agents in the Realm of International Politics:

Double agents often operate in the realm of international politics, influencing diplomatic relations and shaping the course of history. This subchapter examines the role of double agents in political espionage, exploring their impact on international affairs and the delicate balance of power between nations.

Technological Espionage Stories:

The Secret Lives of Double Agents in the Cyber Age:

With the rise of the digital era, double agents have adapted their methods to exploit technological vulnerabilities. This subchapter uncovers the secret lives of double agents operating in the cyber age, where information is a weapon, and the line between the physical and virtual world blurs.

Femme Fatale Espionage Stories:

Double Agents and the Art of Seduction:

The art of seduction has long been a powerful tool in espionage. This subchapter delves into the captivating stories of femme fatale double agents, who used their charm and allure to extract valuable information and manipulate their targets. Their stories highlight the dangerous intersection of love, loyalty, and betrayal.

Conclusion:

Double agents are the unsung heroes of counterintelligence operations. Their stories, as explored in "Masters of Deceit: Double Agents and the Dangerous Game of Counterintelligence," captivate readers across various niches. Whether it's the intrigue of Cold War espionage, the historical allure of double agents, or the high-stakes adventures of modern spy thrillers, the dangerous game of counterintelligence promises to enthrall readers from all walks of life.

Real-Life Stories of Double Agents Caught in the Act

In the riveting subchapter titled "Real-Life Stories of Double Agents Caught in the Act," the book "Masters of Deceit: Double Agents and the Dangerous Game of Counterintelligence" takes readers on a thrilling journey into the clandestine world of espionage. Drawing from the annals of history and contemporary events, this chapter sheds light on the treacherous lives of double agents who played a dangerous game of deceit.

For the lovers of Cold War espionage stories, this subchapter delves into the intricate world of double agents during the Cold War era. It uncovers the shadowy figures who walked the thin line between loyalty and betrayal, risking their lives to gather intelligence for both sides of the conflict.

Historical espionage enthusiasts will be captivated by the unveiling of double agents throughout history. From ancient civilizations to modern times, the book recounts the lives of these mysterious figures who operated in the shadows, shaping the course of events with their double-edged actions.

For those seeking high-stakes adventures, the subchapter explores spy thriller espionage stories. It unravels the heart-pounding tales of double agents in the modern world, where technology and global politics collide, and the consequences of their actions can change the course of history.

Political enthusiasts will be engrossed in the realm of international politics, where double agents lurk in the shadows. This chapter sheds light on the secretive world of political espionage, where double agents maneuver between rival nations, manipulating events to their advantage.

In the age of technology, the subchapter on technological espionage stories offers a glimpse into the secret lives of double agents in the cyber age. It explores the dangerous game of counterintelligence played out in the digital realm, where information is power, and one wrong move can have catastrophic consequences.

For those intrigued by the art of seduction, the subchapter on femme fatale espionage stories uncovers the dangerous liaisons of double agents. It delves into the seductive tactics employed by these spies, using their charm and allure to extract vital information from unsuspecting targets.

Lastly, this subchapter explores the treacherous world of undercover operations. It reveals the dangerous game of counterintelligence, where double agents risk their lives to infiltrate enemy organizations, gathering vital intelligence while constantly evading detection.

In "Real-Life Stories of Double Agents Caught in the Act," readers will be captivated by the thrilling tales of double agents operating in the murky world of espionage. Whether you are a history buff, a lover of spy thrillers, or simply someone fascinated by the dangerous game of counterintelligence, this subchapter offers a captivating glimpse into the secret lives of double agents throughout history.

Chapter 8: The Treacherous World of Undercover Operations: Double Agents in Action

Infiltrating Enemy Lines: The Life of an Undercover Double Agent

In the shadowy world of espionage, few roles are as perilous and intriguing as that of an undercover double agent. These individuals navigate treacherous waters, playing a dangerous game of deception, loyalty, and betrayal. In "Masters of Deceit: Double Agents and the Dangerous Game of Counterintelligence," we delve into the clandestine lives of these unsung heroes, exploring their tales of courage, cunning, and sacrifice.

During the Cold War era, the intricate world of double agents reached its zenith. Operating on the front lines of the ideological battle between the East and the West, these spies risked everything for the cause they believed in. Their stories, told for the first time, will captivate Cold War espionage enthusiasts who yearn for a deeper understanding of this riveting era.

But the history of double agents is not confined to the Cold War. Throughout history, brave men and women have walked the tightrope of deception, gathering intelligence and thwarting enemy plans. From World War II to the present day, we explore the lives of these historical double agents, shedding light on their motivations and the impact they had on shaping the course of events.

In the modern world, the stakes have never been higher. As technology advances, so too does the realm of espionage. Our book takes you into the heart of the cyber age, where double agents now operate in the shadows of the digital world. Discover the secret lives of these technological spies, as they navigate the intricate web of information, constantly evolving to outwit their adversaries.

But it's not just technology that shapes the world of double agents. The art of seduction has long been a powerful tool in the spy's arsenal. Femme fatales have played a pivotal role in espionage throughout history, using their charm and allure to extract vital secrets. We delve into their fascinating stories, uncovering the dangerous game of seduction played by these remarkable individuals.

For those with a taste for political intrigue, our book shines a light on the murky world of double agents in the realm of international politics. From the highest echelons of power to the darkest corners of espionage, we explore the complex web of loyalties and betrayals that shape the geopolitical landscape.

Join us on a thrilling journey through the dangerous game of counterintelligence, as we unveil the lives of undercover double agents. From the treacherous Cold War era to the modern cyber age, their stories will leave you breathless, reminding us that truth and deception are often two sides of the same coin in the world of espionage.

The Thrills and Dangers of Undercover Missions

In the realm of espionage, undercover missions are the heart-pounding moments that make for gripping stories and unforgettable adventures. From the Cold War era to the modern world, double agents have played a dangerous game of deception, infiltrating enemy lines and gathering critical intelligence. However, with high stakes come great risks, and the life of a double agent is fraught with danger.

For those enamored with Cold War espionage stories, the intricate world of double agents during this era is sure to captivate. From the tension-filled exchanges at the Berlin Wall to the nail-biting encounters in the back alleys of Moscow, these stories reveal the true extent of the danger faced by those who dared to cross enemy lines.

Delving into historical espionage stories, readers will be taken on a journey through time, unveiling the lives of double agents throughout history. From ancient Rome to World War II, these tales shed light on the sacrifices made by these brave individuals and the impact they had on shaping the course of events.

For those seeking high-stakes adventures in the modern world, spy thriller espionage stories offer an adrenaline rush like no other. Think covert operations in the heart of enemy territory, daring escapes from hostile agents, and the constant threat of betrayal. These stories remind us that the world of double agents is as thrilling and dangerous as ever.

The realm of international politics provides a unique backdrop for political espionage stories. In this arena, double agents navigate treacherous waters, working to protect their countries' interests while concealing their true loyalties. These stories offer a glimpse into a world where trust is a rare commodity and betrayal can have far-reaching consequences.

In the cyber age, technological espionage stories take center stage. Double agents skilled in hacking, encryption, and cyber warfare operate in the shadows, stealing valuable information and sabotaging enemy systems. These stories shed light on the secret lives of these modern-day spies and the ever-evolving landscape of espionage.

Femme fatale espionage stories explore the art of seduction as a powerful tool in the hands of double agents. These agents use their charm and allure to extract secrets from unsuspecting targets, blurring the line between love and betrayal. These stories reveal the dangerous game of cat and mouse played by double agents skilled in the art of manipulation.

In the treacherous world of undercover operations, espionage stories expose the perils faced by double agents on a daily basis. From the constant fear of discovery to the emotional toll of living a life of lies, these stories delve into the psychological and physical challenges of this dangerous game.

In conclusion, the thrills and dangers of undercover missions are at the core of the captivating world of double agents. From the Cold War era to the modern cyber age, these stories offer a glimpse into a realm where deception, danger, and high-stakes adventures reign supreme. Whether you're a fan of historical intrigue, political maneuvering, or pulse-pounding action, the world of double agents has something to offer for every niche. Brace yourself for a thrilling ride into the dangerous game of counterintelligence.

The Sacrifices and Moral Dilemmas Faced by Double Agents

In the shadows of the Cold War era, a dangerous game of counterintelligence unfolded, with double agents at the heart of the action. These masters of deceit navigated a treacherous world where loyalty was a luxury and betrayal ran rampant. But behind their cunning façades, these double agents faced sacrifices and moral dilemmas that shaped their lives and the course of history.

For the public, these stories offer a glimpse into the intricate world of Cold War espionage. From Berlin to Moscow, from Washington D.C. to London, these double agents operated on the razor's edge, torn between their loyalty to their home country and their allegiance to the enemy they infiltrated. Their ability to maintain this delicate balance came at a great personal cost. Many had to abandon their families, leaving behind loved ones who could never know the truth. The sacrifices they made weighed heavily on their conscience, as they lived a life of constant lies and deception.

But the moral dilemmas faced by these double agents went beyond their personal lives. They were confronted with decisions that would impact not just their own fate, but also the outcome of global conflicts. In the realm of international politics, where the stakes were high, they had to make split-second choices that could mean life or death for countless individuals. Their actions had the power to reshape the course of history, but at what price?

As the world evolved, so did the double agents' challenges. In the cyber age, these spies had to adapt to a new battleground, where technology became their weapon of choice. They faced a moral dilemma of a different kind – choosing between the greater good and the potential destruction that their actions in the digital realm could unleash.

Moreover, the art of seduction was a powerful tool in the hands of double agents. Femme fatales deployed their charm and allure to extract valuable information from unsuspecting targets. Yet, behind their glamorous facade, they too faced moral dilemmas. How far were they willing to go in the name of their mission? And what toll did their actions take on their own sense of morality?

In the dangerous game of counterintelligence, double agents walked a tightrope between loyalty and betrayal, sacrifice and personal gain. Their stories are a testament to the complex nature of espionage and the human spirit. As we delve into their tales, we are reminded of the sacrifices they made, the moral dilemmas they faced, and the lasting impact they had on the world of espionage.

The Legacy of Double Agents in the World of Espionage

Double agents have long been a captivating and enigmatic presence in the world of espionage. These individuals, who operate on the razor's edge between truth and deceit, have played a crucial role in shaping the course of history. In the book "Masters of Deceit: Double Agents and the

Dangerous Game of Counterintelligence," we delve into the intriguing lives of these shadowy figures and explore the lasting impact they have had on the world.

Cold War Espionage Stories: The Intricate World of Double Agents during the Cold War Era

During the Cold War, the battle between the East and the West reached new heights of intensity. Double agents became invaluable assets in this high-stakes game of espionage, infiltrating enemy ranks and providing vital intelligence to their handlers. Their actions often determined the outcome of critical events, such as the Cuban Missile Crisis and the Berlin Wall's construction.

Historical Espionage Stories: Unveiling the Lives of Double Agents Throughout History

While the Cold War era may be the most well-known period for double agents, their presence extends far beyond that. Throughout history, these individuals have operated in various contexts, from ancient civilizations to modern times. We uncover the stories of double agents such as Mata Hari and Kim Philby, shedding light on their motivations and the consequences of their actions.

Spy Thriller Espionage Stories: High-Stakes Adventures of Double Agents in the Modern World

In today's interconnected world, the game of espionage continues to evolve. The stories of modern double agents read like thrilling spy novels, filled with high-stakes adventures and heart-pounding action. We explore the exploits of double agents operating in the shadows of the intelligence community, battling against formidable adversaries while risking their own lives.

Political Espionage Stories: Double Agents in the Realm of International Politics

Political espionage is a dangerous game, with double agents playing a pivotal role in shaping international relations. These individuals maneuver through the corridors of power, manipulating political landscapes and influencing key decision-makers. We delve into the intricate web of political espionage, revealing the complex motivations driving double agents and the far-reaching consequences of their actions.

Technological Espionage Stories: The Secret Lives of Double Agents in the Cyber Age

In the digital age, the battleground of espionage has expanded into cyberspace. Double agents now operate in the realm of technological espionage, using their insider knowledge to exploit vulnerabilities and extract valuable information. We explore the clandestine world of cyber spies, shedding light on their methods and the devastating impact they can have on individuals, organizations, and nations.

Femme Fatale Espionage Stories: Double Agents and the Art of Seduction

Throughout history, double agents have harnessed the power of seduction to extract sensitive information from unsuspecting targets. These femme fatales use their charm, beauty, and wit to manipulate their way into the inner circles of power. We uncover the hidden stories of these seductive double agents, examining the complexities of their roles and the dangerous games they play.

Espionage Stories: Double Agents and the Dangerous Game of Counterintelligence

The world of counterintelligence is a treacherous one, with double agents at its heart. These individuals navigate a dangerous tightrope, constantly balancing their loyalty to their handlers with their desire to protect their true identity. We delve into the dangerous game of counterintelligence, exploring the challenges faced by double agents and the risks they take to maintain their cover.

Espionage Stories: Double Agents and the Treacherous World of Undercover Operations

Undercover operations are the epitome of espionage, requiring double agents to immerse themselves in enemy territory while maintaining their true allegiance. These covert operatives face constant danger and must rely on their wit, resourcefulness, and ability to adapt to survive. We unveil the thrilling world of undercover operations, shedding light on the harrowing experiences of double agents and the impact they have on global security.

In "Masters of Deceit: Double Agents and the Dangerous Game of Counterintelligence," we explore the legacy of double agents and their enduring impact on the world of espionage. These intriguing stories appeal to a wide range of audiences, from history enthusiasts to fans of spy thrillers. Join us as we uncover the secrets and unravel the fascinating lives of these mysterious figures.

Conclusion: The Legacy of Double Agents: Lessons from the Dangerous Game of Counterintelligence

In the world of espionage, the role of double agents is both fascinating and treacherous. Throughout history, these enigmatic figures have played a pivotal role in shaping the outcomes of conflicts and wars. In "Masters of Deceit: Double Agents and the Dangerous Game of Counterintelligence," we have delved into the intricate lives of double agents during the Cold War era and beyond, unveiling their secrets and shedding light on their dangerous game of counterintelligence.

For the public, this book offers a thrilling peek into the shadowy world of espionage. Cold War espionage stories have captivated the public imagination for decades, and we have explored the lives of double agents who risked everything to serve their countries, often at great personal cost. These historical espionage stories provide valuable insights into the sacrifices and betrayals that occurred during this tumultuous period of history.

In the modern world, the stakes are higher than ever, and the game of counterintelligence has evolved. Spy thriller espionage stories have become a staple of popular culture, and we have examined the high-stakes adventures of double agents in this ever-changing landscape. The realm of international politics is rife with intrigue, and political espionage stories shed light on the complex relationships between nations and the role double agents play in shaping these dynamics.

With the advent of technology, a new form of espionage has emerged. Technological espionage stories have unveiled the secret lives of double agents in the cyber age. These stories serve as cautionary tales, reminding us of the vulnerabilities and threats posed by the digital era.

In the realm of undercover operations, double agents have often used the art of seduction to achieve their objectives. Femme fatale espionage stories explore the intricate world of double agents and the power of manipulation and seduction. These stories highlight the dangerous game of counterintelligence and the lengths to which double agents will go to achieve their goals.

In conclusion, the world of double agents and counterintelligence is a treacherous one, filled with danger and intrigue. The legacy of these individuals is a testament to the complexity of human nature and the lengths to which people will go to protect their beliefs and ideals. Whether in the context of Cold War espionage, historical events, modern spy thrillers, political intrigue, technological advancements, or the art of seduction, double agents have left an indelible mark on the world of espionage. As we navigate the complexities of the present and future, these lessons from the dangerous game of counterintelligence should serve as a reminder of the ever-present need for vigilance and caution in the face of hidden threats.